A LOVE OF THE LAKES

A LOVE OF THE LAKES

Photographs by Geoffrey Berry
Text by Brian Redhead

Constable · London

First published in Great Britain 1988
by Constable and Company Limited
10 Orange Street London WC2H 7EG
Copyright © 1988 text by Brian Redhead
Copyright © 1988 photographs by the estate of Geoffrey Berry
Reprinted 1989
Set in Monophoto Photina 11pt by
BAS Printers Limited, Over Wallop, Hampshire
Printed and bound in Spain by
Graficas Estella, S.A.

For

MOLLY BERRY

Contents

Geoffrey Berry
1912–1988

I first clapped eyes on Geoffrey Berry in 1966 at an exhibition of his photographs at Abbot Hall in Kendal. I was no stranger to his work because I had often used it to adorn the feature pages of the *Guardian*. I was no stranger to his ideas because it was the practice along the Corridor in Cross Street to consult him before writing yet another leading article on access to Thirlmere.

But it was when I came face to face with his photographs laid out in sequence round these rooms that I realized that here was a man who not only saw but understood. I said so to the assembly at the time. And afterwards Geoffrey approached me with that shy sidelong look of his, thanked me, then, colouring slightly, begged me not to overdo my praise.

He was a modest man who had much to be immodest about. For many people, for many years, he *was* the Lake District – its voice, its conscience, its protector. Wainwright charted it; Geoffrey defended it. Whenever anyone was about to do something in the Lakes which ought not to be done, Geoffrey was there, listening, noting, correcting, and quietly admonishing.

But for him and the Friends of the Lake District, whom he served as secretary and then as consultant, there would probably be powerboats now on Ullswater and Derwentwater and Coniston, heavy traffic still rumbling up and down the A591, and ugly rims round the fallen levels of Ennerdale Water and Wastwater. Geoffrey's rueful account of *The Tale of Two Lakes* is a masterpiece of quiet

victory. And his account with Geoffrey Beard of *A Century of Conservation* in the Lake District is the most knowledgeable account of the battle so far.

In any conflict of interests in the Lake District Geoffrey was always the best man to have on your side. He was courteous to opponents, gracious in victory and in defeat, scholarly throughout. He could argue a case with such precision and truthfulness that even those whose arguments he had thoughtfully demolished would acknowledge his virtues. The only person I ever heard say something harsh about him was a developer in the last throes of incoherence whom Geoffrey had left without a leg to stand on.

Not that Geoffrey was sanguine; quite the opposite. He feared for the future of his beloved Lakes, aware that every destroyer repelled made way for another attack. Though he worked closely with the National Park Authority, he sometimes had his doubts about their militancy, and very serious doubts about the intentions of central government. But every photograph he took, and he took one or more most days, was an affirmation of his love of the Lakes.

He and I had not been in touch for some time when circumstances brought us together in the Lakes on several occasions in 1987. On the day of the annual general meeting of the Friends of the Lake District we met for lunch. Geoffrey had with him a copy of the book *Northumbria* which is made up of a collection of photographs by David Bell and a recollection of my days there. He was characteristically kind about it.

'You and I should do one,' I suggested. 'We could call it *A Love of the Lakes*.'

He gave me his sidelong look and smiled. 'Yes we could,' he said. So we set about it.

He and his wife Molly put together a collection of his favourite colour photographs, taken in all his favourite places in the Lakes, often with Molly in them, as she said, to provide scale. They sent them to Constable soon after Christmas, and in early January I called to inspect them. I enthused, the publisher phoned Geoffrey, and we planned a meeting in Kendal.

It never took place. Geoffrey died the day after the telephone conversation. *The Times* in its obituary column dubbed him Defender of the Lakes; the *Independent* called him 'an active and devoted enthusiast'; the *Westmorland Gazette*, 'a crusading Lakeland conservationist'.

In a letter to the publisher Geoffrey had written: 'I have selected some photographs not for their artistic or scenic qualities but because they show something interesting about the Lake District.' Molly, who was busy collecting information for the captions to underline that interest, said in her sorrow that she was happy for the project to proceed.

In his last letter to me, in reply to my suggestion that we should think of extending the boundaries of the Lake District National Park, he reminded me that we, or rather he and his Friends, already had. 'In 1972,' he wrote, 'we put forward the ambitious scheme of extending the eastern boundary to include the Borrowbeck Valley, the northern Howgills, and that part of the Yorkshire Dales National Park which is now in Cumbria. Since then we have been more moderate and advocated an extension to the east to include Borrowbeck Valley to the M6, as well as additions in the south to include Brigsteer and the Cartmel peninsula.'

At the very least, we owe it to his memory to achieve that.

B.R.

TIME AND TIME AGAIN

When I was ten, and an evacuee, I found myself in the front bedroom of Mrs Taylor's council house at the top of Inglewood Road in Penrith. It was school policy to billet fee-paying pupils with owner-occupiers and the scholarship boys with council tenants. So Harry Myers and I were Mrs Taylor's contribution to the war effort and for four years we occupied her best bedroom.

It had the best view of any council-house bedroom in Britain. High up on the Fair Hill in the shadow of the Beacon, it looked out on to the Lake District. 'That', said Harry, who had looked it up, 'is Saddleback.' And I have never called it Blencathra from that day to this.

It was not my first view of the Lake District. Two or three years earlier from our home in Newcastle we – my father, my mother and I – had set out in my father's new Austin Seven, registration number BVK 966, for the Lakes. We stopped our baby Austin, I recall, on Hartside for me to be photographed by a baby Brownie. It was a small world.

Our plan was to drive to Ullswater, but my father was an irascible man. When he took a wrong turning he was not one to be turned back, and my mother knew when to hold her tongue. So when we missed the turn for Pooley Bridge we found ourselves at Haweswater. My mother was very disappointed but not I. I had never seen a dam before and I ran along the top of it whooping with delight. A water engineer shouted at me to desist but fell silent when my father, who had once fought Cast Iron Casey the Sunderland Assassin, frowned upon him.

I did not know then that Mardale lay beneath that drinking water, but forty-five years later, when the man-made lake ran dry, I stood on the little humped-back bridge in the middle of the village unexpectedly exposed once more to the sunshine and told a TV cameraman about my earlier visit. He was not very impressed, never having heard of Cast Iron Casey, but he was astonished to find a beauty spot in the Lake District not disfigured by the relics of previous camera crews. 'Where', he asked, 'are the holes made by the feet of earlier tripods?' A question worth a series in itself.

But I am ahead of myself. The moment Harry Myers and I set eyes on Saddleback we vowed to visit it. This was not as easy as it might appear. We only had one bicycle between us – mine. And I had parked it by the kerb outside the chip shop in Drover's Lane. It had fallen into the road, whereupon it was run over by a passing lorry. I had gone to the police station to protest but there was no justice in those days, and I was now saving up for a new wheel.

However, Mrs Taylor's youngest son, a plump lazy cheerful man who had escaped conscription because his eyes were bad, offered to drive us up to Saddleback next time his work as a telephone engineer took him there. There were, I realize now, no telephones on Saddleback then, and no telephone lines ran up it. But nonetheless we went, squashed in the back of his little green van, to visit every inch of the telephone territory controlled by Penrith.

Then when I got a new wheel and Harry got a bike of his own – half a crown from a dubious dealer in Dockray Square – the Lake District was our playground. We cycled everywhere, made light even of Kirkstone Pass, and meticulously recorded, as small boys will, everything we saw and learned. We had lists of journeys accomplished, miles covered, altitudes achieved, flora and fauna spotted, sweet coupons consumed.

Poetry came with puberty. We cycled more slowly, and talked about the sunset and about Iris, the daughter of the publican in the pub opposite the chip shop in Drover's Lane. Harry, who already knew the first book of Virgil's *Aeneid* off by heart in Latin, vowed to learn the whole of Wordsworth's ode, 'Intimations of Immortality from Recollections of Early Childhood'. Not to be beaten I vowed to write my own 'Intimations' and to get it published in the school magazine, *The Novo*.

But before either of us could complete these tasks, evacuation came to an end. In the summer of 1944 we went home to Newcastle – to trolley buses, to School Certificate, to the prospect of National Service. Some of the parents of fee-paying pupils still had cottages in the Lake District, but for the scholarship boys it was a memory of childhood. When Harry married he and his wife chose to call their first home 'Blencathra'.

It was twenty years before I returned to the Lake District to reside. As a reporter I had popped in and out, but rarely stayed for more than a night or two, and my wife was reluctant in those days to holiday in the Lakes. She too had been an evacuee, billeted in a school boarding-house in Ambleside and turfed out every day from dawn to dusk to walk the fells on little eleven-year-old legs. It took her time to discover that there is more to

the Lakes than water in your wellies and hunger in your heart.

But in the summer of '63 we took a holiday in the Lodore Swiss Hotel on Derwentwater and it all came alive again. We were living in London then but two years later I was moved back to Manchester, and on the very day that was made known I had a phone call from a friend asking me if I would like a cottage in the Lakes. 'Yes,' I said without hesitation, and signed a tenancy agreement without even seeing the place.

And so it came about that at Easter 1966 we found ourselves – and we were a family of six – comfortable in a cottage at Grassthwaitehow, sitting in the sunshine on the front doorstep and looking out towards St Sunday Crag and Dollywaggon Pike.

We went to church that Easter at Patterdale, where the vicar was a man of gentle faith and unrestrained enthusiasms. (He had once been the chaplain at the British Embassy in Moscow.) He wished us all 'a simply marvellous Easter' and had us all sing: 'The hills are alive with the sound of music' – a hymn which may have surprised Cranmer but would have delighted Wesley.

The next seven years were years of discovery. We spent every school holiday at the cottage and explored almost everything that the Lakes had to offer. Every day was an expedition, even if we went no further than Lanty's Tarn which stood above our cottage and was the source of our water. We thought of it as our crow's nest, our vantage point, and looked askance at any strangers we found there, until they introduced themselves.

I kept no diary but I have only to hear a name mentioned and I can recall a visit there, or more often many visits there. We went to Patterdale and Glenridding every day for milk and papers, sometimes if it was raining in the car or else on foot down the Milk Path, a steep incline where the children had secret routes and hidden dens.

We stopped a hundred times in Dockray to visit the craft shop, to explore the beck, to tiptoe into the tiny church. We picnicked a thousand times on the edge of Ullswater at Gowbarrow, leaving no litter, and leaving time also to look again at Aira Force.

We went along the other side of the lake to Martindale, the smallest parish in England with two churches, and we preferred the older of the two, St Martin's.

We knew the difference between Troutbeck and Troutbeck, the one on our route back from Keswick dropping down to Dockray, the other, the more famous, on our chosen road back from Windermere. We marvelled at Townend many times from outside, before one day we finally went in and were not disappointed. It really is the finest example of a yeoman farmer's house.

On our journeys to and from the Lakes we took the other road to Kirkstone, the right turn at Ings along what we called our secret route. Never once when we were travelling towards Grassthwaitehow was Kirkstone blocked with snow, though several times snow prevented our return that way, which was no hardship. We did once climb Kirkstone backwards when for some unaccountable reason none of the forward gears in a Rover 2000 would engage, but that may have had something to do with my driving.

We climbed Wrynose and Hard Knott in a great box of a car with a huge bonnet, and halfway up were convinced it was going to fall over backwards. But the Roman fort made it all worth while, and we went back many times.

We knew the difference between Great Langdale and Little Langdale and could name all the summits. We liked the Vale of St John and Mungrisedale, Skelwith Bridge and the far side of Grasmere, we liked Seatoller and Honister and both sides of Bassenthwaite. And we stopped everywhere.

There was no town or village in the Lake District that we did not explore. We knew Boot and Bootle, Backbarrow and Underbarrow, Hartsop and Hawkshead. We knew the difference between Grisedale and Grizedale, between Satterthwaite and Seathwaite, between Ulpha and alpha – top marks.

These daily excursions were not mere diversions to occupy the time nor were they a programme of activities self-consciously devised and accomplished. They were the good life. This was the place to be and these were the things to do in it.

We returned every school holiday as if we had been in exile. Home was home, school was busy, life was full, but this was different. This was the Lakes. This was unchanging. This was a set of values that were constant and dependable. We came to relish the seasons, to make sure it was all intact, and to restore ourselves.

There was a period when I was having a difficult time at my newspaper, locked in an interminable dispute not made any easier by my own recalcitrance. In one moment of frustration I vented my feelings and then grew penitent. I rang the general secretary of the trade union to explain my behaviour. 'What should I do now?' I asked. 'Flee the country,' he replied. Instead I drove up to the Lakes and forgot all about my troubles.

One summer holiday when as far as I can remember it never rained, I read in the warmth of every evening Mary Moorman's two-volume biography of Wordsworth, the only book which does credit to his later years as well as to the years of the famous poems. Every day, between each chapter, we visited the places he had attended – the school at Hawkshead, the various homes, the favourite walks. It was like living his life again.

And we never tired. Colleagues at the office in Manchester would say: 'You are not going to the Lakes again?' And the answer was always, 'Yes.' We did holiday further afield, on Arran and in Sutherland, even once at Bexhill-on-Sea, but Battle and the Conqueror were no substitute for Kendal and Catherine Parr so we scurried back.

It was not a return to the familiar but a return to the infinite. The Lake District is not only the most beautiful part of England, it is also the richest. There is more to the square yard in the Lakes than anywhere – more to see, more to treasure, more to think about.

My eldest son as he grew older took to walking the fells alone. He was immaculate in his preparation – waxing his boots, reading his Wainwright, checking his compass. He would ask to be dropped at Point A at ten in the morning and to be collected at Point B at five in the afternoon. We could drop him at ten, drive off to other attractions, and arrive at Point B at five to see him striding confidently down the fell, accurate to the minute.

Once he was on Crinkle Crags when the mist descended. Properly prepared, he knew the way and when he came upon a couple of teachers who were lost he led them safely down to Dungeon Ghyll. They asked him who he was and hearing his surname deduced who his father was. 'Your father should be ashamed,' they said, 'letting a young boy like you out on the fells alone.' He was outraged. He had led them back to safety, and he was all for taking them back and leaving them alone.

His younger brother liked visiting farms best. His favourite day of the year was the day of the Patterdale Show. He could watch sheepdog trials for hours. Once when the television screened a programme about a year in the life of a hill farmer he sat in front of the set for an hour without speaking or moving. When the programme ended he took his thumb out of his mouth and pronounced judgement. 'That', he said, 'was the best programme ever shown.' And with that he went to bed.

This was the time when the M6 was approaching the Lake District and there were fears that the coming torrent of visitors would flood the Lakes. Could they be diverted? I was serving at the time on the board of the British Tourist Authority and I tried to persuade the Disney organization to build a Disneyland at Morecambe. That, I said, would divert the day trippers. Disney was keen and Morecambe was keen but it came to nothing.

So I devised instead a great plan to build a whole holiday complex at Killington, the service station on the M6 not far from Junction 37 where the Kendal to Sedbergh road crosses the motorway. The idea was to increase the size of the lake there, which I think was done, and then to build a holiday village which would have everything except somewhere to stay. You would bring your own accommodation – a tent or a trailer caravan or a motor caravan. These would assemble in three separate parks (rather than in the Lake District) and the new village would provide not only water sports and grass ski-ing, but indoor facilities too, shopping, bistros, bars, and even a theatre.

Many people enthused until the Water Resources Board announced that it might be necessary one day to flood the valley to provide another reservoir and my scheme sank without trace. The reservoir has never been built but (unlike Mardale) Camp 37, I fear, will never surface. Which, come to think of it, may be no bad thing. Today I would be opposed to the very idea of such a development so close to the Lakes, which I take to be a sign of wisdom and not just of age.

We lived half way up Helvellyn for those seven years, but I never went to the top. I knew it was there and needed no further proof. In any case my children returned with regular reports of its continuing existence. Their eyes had been opened by our neighbour.

The cottage we rented belonged to the Ullswater Foxhounds and the huntsman, Joe Wear, lived next door to us. He was to be a greater influence upon the children, especially the eldest, than any teacher. Almost the first time that my eldest son was taken for a walk by Mr Wear, he returned and solemnly announced that when he grew up he was going to work in the jungle with wild animals. Fifteen years later he was counting monkeys in Peru.

Mr Wear, as the children always called him, was a countryman like no other. He had been a huntsman all his working life, and hunting in the Lake District is not a social sport but a social service. Hunting is on foot and by subscription pack. Farmers subscribe a hound to the pack and summon the huntsman when foxes are harrying their lambs. When the hounds pursue the fox, the huntsman walks the foot of the fell, his number two, the Whip, walks high up the fell and they keep the pack between them. Terriers complete the task force.

Mr Wear had favourite hounds, favourite terriers, and favourite foxes. There were some foxes so cunning that he admired their skills and allowed them to escape. One, I remember, lay crouched on a window sill as the pack hastened through the farmyard. Mr Wear strode past too, pausing only to wink at the fox. His favourite terrier was Nettle, a fearsome little dog with one tooth. Were you to raise a hand to Nettle, he would cheerfully bite your throat. Mr Wear loved him like a pet, and when Nettle was savaged by a badger, which picked him up in its teeth and smashed him against a wall, Mr Wear was heartbroken.

Mr Wear's vegetable garden was next to our cottage. Moles would enter it, burrowing beneath the neat rows of lettuce, and pull the plants down in their pursuit of worms. Mr Wear disapproved of such behaviour, and often of an evening we would see him walk grimly past our door with a shotgun crooked beneath his arm. He would poke the barrel into the ground at one end of the lettuce row and wait. The lettuces would disappear in sequence as the mole made its way unwittingly towards its end. Mr Wear would pull the trigger and the mole was done for.

Mr Wear had walked every inch of the Eastern fells. Nothing escaped him. 'Sit down and be quiet,' he would say, 'a badger is coming.' And a badger would come. Recalling those days, my eldest son says that Mr Wear talked about the fells like no one else. He mentioned neither their names nor their summits. He talked instead about every knoll and every ghyll and named them all. For him the fells were not summits to be climbed, like badges to be collected or awards to be won, but landscapes to be lived on and loved.

I remember once finding him watching the Queen at some ceremony on television. 'Pity that poor woman,' he said, 'having to shake hands with all those people. I'd rather be up Helvellyn talking to myself.' Or as he put it, 'me-sel'.

He was wicked with visitors. Townees, he called them. He would pretend not wholly to understand what they asked, offer them misleading information, and chuckle at the thought that they would subsequently misinform everyone they met.

And he loved gossip, He would tell tales of the departed that Hugh Walpole never dreamt of. My favourite was the story, which I knew to be true, of the woman who played the organ at the local church. Her husband had been something of a philanderer, and when he died she played the organ at his funeral in the morning and at a wedding in the church that afternoon.

When Mr Wear died we set off as a family for the church at Patterdale. But the M6 was crowded and when we arrived the church was full and the service about to start. We joined the even greater congregation outside, comforted that so many had thought fit to be present.

By then we no longer lived at Grassthwaitehow. We pretended that we had been cruelly evicted but in truth we had gracefully surrendered the tenancy when Mr Wear retired so that Mrs Wear could stay in their house and the new huntsman have ours. By then also our children had other things to do – competitive games to play, concerts to play in, their own lives to lead.

For three summers we rented holiday houses on one side of Windermere or the other, happy to be in the heart of Lakeland, but it was never quite the same. We felt like visitors again, not residents.

We did consider taking a house at Ramsteads, a ramshackle development in an estate off the road between Outgate and the Drunken Duck. It was built by Michael Boddington, seventh son of a brewery, and a great Hurricane pilot in the Second World War. He had no time for planners (although his son was one) and he built his little settlement, which was not unlike an estate of gingerbread houses, without the benefit of planning permission. When the planners protested he reached for a shotgun and ordered them off his land. When they returned with the constabulary he took himself off, and that Christmas I had a card from him from the Cook Islands in the South Pacific. He said he thought little of authority there too.

Once we had surrendered the cottage our visits to the Lakes became less frequent. But we spent many happy and gregarious evenings at 'Michael's Nook', free to gossip, and freed of the washing up. I had long had a hand, or more accurately a voice, in various happenings in the Lakes, often to do with Wordsworth. I once refused an invitation to Number 10 rather than miss the first and probably the only performance of Wordsworth's play, *The Borderers*.

I spoke at many functions in the Lakes, usually to open an exhibition, often to raise money for a good cause. And there is no better cause than the creation of some activity which will further enrich life in the Lakes. The Lake District Summer School of Music is the latest example, a gathering of some of the best young musicians in the land once a year, with performances, to which the public are welcome, by the attending teachers. One of the most memorable evenings for me was in Ambleside Parish Church when I introduced a performance of music by Mozart and Schubert by the Franz Schubert Quartet from Vienna. Coleridge would have enjoyed that.

Lately I have been caught up in what may be called the politics of the Lakes. I brought it upon myself by allowing my name to go forward as President of the Council for National Parks. But I don't regret it. The Lakes are too popular to be left to the populists, let alone to the populace. They need real friends, who value them for what they are, to restrain those who see them simply as a resort or a business opportunity. Lovers of the Lakes do not need to be told what is good for the Lake District and what is not. Their instincts will tell them. But for the others it has to be said out loud, and often.

To love the Lakes is to understand that the Lake District cannot be encompassed in a single adjective. To say that it is beautiful or majestic, solitary or wild, may be true but it is not enough. The Lake District is not just scenery or background, it is a wonder of creation. To love it is not a sentimental fancy but a moral judgement, on it and on us.

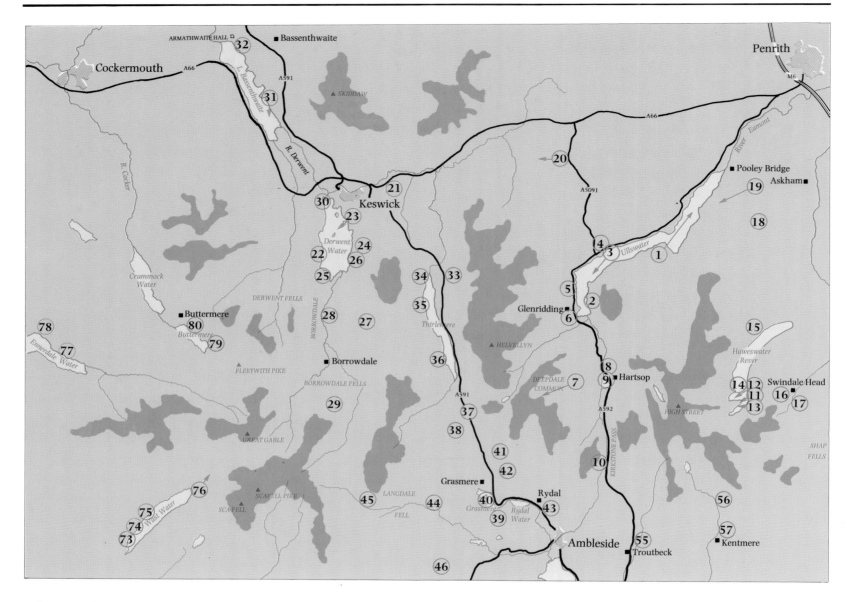

The Lake District

The North East

1 Ullswater from Hallin Fell
2 Across Ullswater from its eastern shore
3 Silver Point from Ullswater's western shore
4 Sheffield Pike from Aira Point
5 Silver Point across Ullswater
6 The Greenside valley from Keldas, Patterdale
7 Fairfield's northern crags from Deepdale
8 Cow Bridge, near Hartsop
9 Brothers' Water

10 The Kirk Stone
11 Harter Fell from Haweswater
12 Haweswater from Whiteacre Crag
13 The Riggindale Ridge across
   Haweswater
14 Chapel Bridge, Mardale, in 1984
15 The Measand Falls, Haweswater
16 The head of Swindale
17 Waterfall in Swindale
18 The Cop Stone, Moor Divock
19 Ancient boundary stone on
   Heughscar Hill

The North

20 Blencathra from the south east
21 Castlerigg Stone Circle
22 Brandlehow, Derwent Water
23 Across Derwent Water to Cat Bells
24 Skiddaw from Derwent Water's
   eastern shore
25 Derwent Water
26 Looking to Rampsholme Island,
   Derwent Water
27 Watendlath Bridge
28 The Jaws of Borrowdale
29 Tarn at Leaves, Borrowdale fells

30 Skiddaw from the foot of Derwent Water
31 From the Eastern shore of Bassenthwaite Lake
32 Skiddaw, Ullock Pike and The Dodd from
   Bassenthwaite Lake
33 Castle Rock, St John's Vale
34 St John's Beck, Thirlmere
35 Across Thirlmere to the Helvellyn ridge
36 Birks Stone, Thirlmere

The Centre

37 Dunmail Raise
38 Helm Crag from the Greenburn valley
39 Grasmere from Loughrigg Terrace

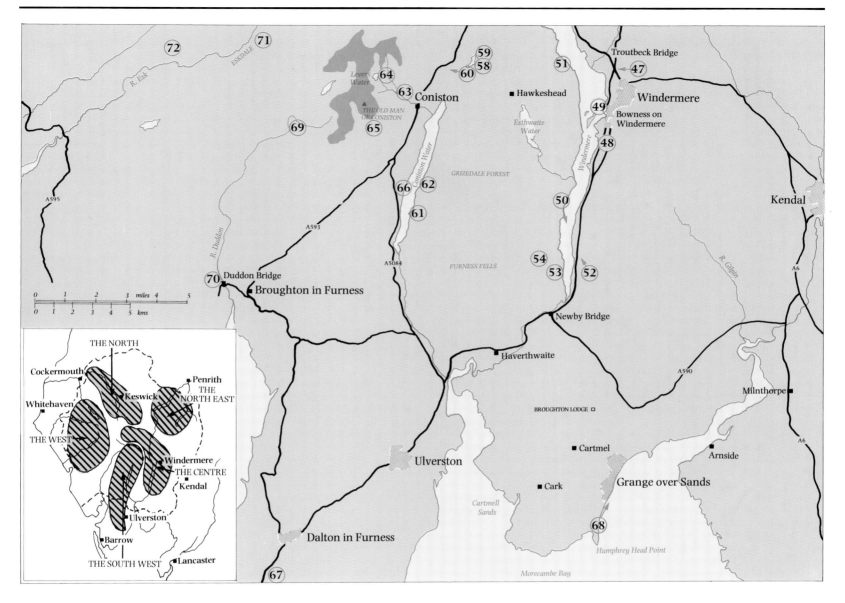

40 Bluebells on Grasmere's island
41 Grasmere village from Grey Crag
42 Alcock Tarn
43 Dora's Field, Rydal
44 The Langdale Pikes
45 Pike of Stickle from Mickleden
46 Little Langdale tarn
47 Orrest Head, Windermere
48 Windermere from Ferry Nab
49 The Round House, Belle Island
50 The western shore of Windermere
51 Windermere and the Fairfield Horseshoe
52 Windermere from Gummers How
53 Stott Park bobbin mill

54 High Dam, Finsthwaite Heights
55 Town Head, Troutbeck
56 Upper Kentmere
57 Packhorse bridge, Kentmere

The South West

58 Tarn Hows
59 Tarn Hows in winter
60 The Tilberthwaite valley and Wetherlam
61 Peel Island, Coniston Water
62 Coniston from the eastern shore
63 The Coppermines Valley, Coniston
64 Levers Water

65 Coniston Old Man from Torver Common
66 Kelly Hall Tarn
67 Furness Abbey
68 The Kent Estuary

The West

69 Seathwaite Bridge, Dunnerdale
70 Duddon Iron Furnace
71 Hardknott Castle Roman fort
72 View across Eskdale
73 Wasdale with Great Gable and the Scafells
74 Wastwater Screes
75 Wastwater with Yewbarrow and Great Gable

76 Great Gable
77 Ennerdale Water with Pillar Mountains
78 Gathering the flock in Ennerdale
79 Buttermere with Fleetwith Pike
80 Haystacks and the head of Buttermere

The North East

Ullswater is the perfect introduction to the Lake District and the best way to it is from the north east. It is the second largest lake in the Lake District, and the most beautiful. When first encountered at Pooley Bridge, Ullswater is set in gentle countryside, but at its head the mountains have closed in, penetrated only by the Kirkstone Pass. Once a stern barrier, the Pass in this motor age is merely considered a steepish road. But Haweswater, the eastern outpost of the Lake District, defeats the motor car. No road makes its way through its crag-ringed head. Haweswater is a reservoir but no less impressive, and in the drought of 1984, when the drowned Mardale reappeared, it was indeed dramatic. Away from Haweswater and its immediate surroundings, this eastern escarpment of the Lake District is little visited. Few go to the beautiful dales of Swindale and Wet Sleddale, and there are vast tracts of lonely moorland. Prehistoric man was here and left his mark. The Romans built a road through this wilderness, but modern man sees it only as the skyline west of the M6, and hurries on. There are those who complain that the Lake District is overcrowded; not this part of it.

(1) Ullswater from Hallin Fell

From Hallin Fell, a rocky knoll rising from the
eastern shore of Ullswater, the view is down
the northern reach of the lake with the snow-
capped Pennines on the far horizon. Between
lies the wide Eden Valley, and it is across this
that the road runs into the north east of the
Lake District. This is a pastoral scene, but it is
looking out of the Lake District. The view
looking up to the head of Ullswater is of a
sterner kind. This is characteristic of the Lake
District. From the central dome of mountains
the lakes, in their glaciated troughs, radiate
out into a more pastoral countryside.

(2) Ullswater in winter

A raft of ice stills the lake waters. On the
skyline, seen across the southern reach of
Ullswater, is St Sunday Crag and Nethermost
Pike, with snow gullies running up to the
Helvellyn ridge. On this eastern side of the lake
there is no motor road beyond Howtown; from
there a bridleway runs to Patterdale at the
head of the lake, and this provides one of the
most delightful walks in the Lake District.

(3) All quiet on Ullswater

On this, the western side of Ullswater, the road
closely follows the shoreline and there are
many secluded bays. Ullswater is a quiet lake.
A speed limit of ten miles per hour ensures that
no noisy motor boats disturb the peace. On the
left, stretching into the lake, is Silver Point.
St Sunday Crag, blocking the valley head, is on
the skyline.

(4) Sheffield Pike

Seen from Aira Point on the western shore of
Ullswater on a winter's day, Sheffield Pike is
against the skyline. It was along these shores
that Wordsworth's daffodils danced. They still
dance here today, as they do in many places
in the Lake District.

(5) Silver Point, Ullswater

Silver Point, here seen from the western shore,
protrudes into the lake. It is the highest section
of what is one of the most beautiful footpaths
in the Lake District. This runs from Howtown
to Patterdale, closely following the water's
edge, at times contouring the steep flanks of
Place Fell, then descending to the lakeside. It
threads its way through woodland and there
are splendid views from the whole of its length.
In summer the lake steamers go close beneath
Silver Point on their way from Glenridding
Pier at the head of Ullswater to Pooley Bridge
at its foot. On the skyline to the right is the
rocky shoulder of Place Fell.

(6) The Greenside Valley

The deep valley of Greenside which runs west
of Glenridding is seen here from the little knott
of Keldas, just above Lanty's Tarn. The valley
was the site of the Greenside Mines which
started in the eighteenth century and were
working until twenty-five years ago. The
extensive tips they left can just be seen on the
valley floor. In recent years great efforts have
been made to restore this shattered valley. The
huge tips have been grassed over and the
derelict mine buildings have either been
demolished or painstakingly repaired. The
Sticks Pass runs up behind the tips on its way
west to St John's Vale.

(7) Deepdale

The brow of Greenhow End dominates the
view up Deepdale. Deepdale is well named;
from the Kirkstone road the path into it is
deceptively level, but it leads to a formidable
cirque of crags. This is the forbidding face of
Fairfield. Fairfield summit is the highest point
in a popular walk, the Fairfield Horseshoe, but
that starts from the other side of the mountain,
not from Deepdale.

(8) Cow Bridge, near Hartsop

Until it was by-passed, this bridge carried the
road from Patterdale to Hartsop and then on
to the Kirkstone Pass. It is now a quiet, shaded
cul-de-sac much favoured as a starting place
for walks up Dovedale and beyond. The peak
in the centre, John Bell's Banner, is the
mountain east of the Kirkstone Pass summit.

(9) Brothers' Water

This is a small lake in a beautiful setting with
the road to the Kirkstone Pass skirting its
eastern shore. It is thought that it was given
the name because of an accident many years
ago when two brothers skating on the lake fell
through the ice and were drowned. In the
centre is the ridge leading up to John Bell's
Banner. The steep path visible on it goes to
some old workings. This must have been a
hard way to earn a living.

(10) The Kirk Stone

This is the boulder which gives the Kirkstone
Pass its name. On the ascent from the
Ullswater side, the stone against the sky has
the appearance of a church tower. It is seen
here looking north. Beyond it the road
descends steeply to Brothers' Water.

(11) Haweswater

Foxgloves bloom above the lake waters and
the craggy face of Harter Fell closes in the dale
head. Haweswater is a reservoir now, but it
maintains its stern beauty. There is no road
beyond the car-park near the head of the lake,
only a bridleway leads by way of the mountain
tarn of Small Water and the steep Nan Bield
Pass into Kentmere. On the right is the wooded
peninsula of The Rigg.

(12) Riggindale, Haweswater

From Whiteacre Crag on the eastern side of
Haweswater, the ridge of Riggindale is seen
across the lake. The path winds over its rocky
tops, Swine Crag, Heron Crag, Eagle Crag and
Rough Crag. From there to the summit of High
Street, which here is seen on the right, is by
the steep ramp of Long Stile. In the coomb
between Riggindale and High Street lies Blea
Tarn, at 207 feet the deepest tarn in the Lake
District.

(13) Storm over Haweswater

The wooded peninsula of The Rigg thrusts out
into the lake. Behind it rises Riggindale, soon
to be engulfed in cloud. The exposed rim on
the opposite shore is typical of reservoirs. In
the drought of 1984 the lake was so drawn
down that it was possible to walk dryshod
across to The Rigg; many people did so.

(14) Chapel Bridge, Mardale:
July 1984

In the drought of 1984 the Haweswater
reservoir fell to its lowest level ever and, fifty
years after it had been drowned, Mardale
reappeared. Although its village, the church
and the inn had been dismantled, their
foundations were still recognizable.
Surprisingly the bridge, after half a century
under water, was still intact and usable. There
is a strange fascination in the re-emergence of
a drowned village and at once Haweswater
became a place of pilgrimage. Television crews
arrived, there were radio programmes and
newspaper articles. So many thousands of
visitors came at weekends that police were
needed to control the flow of traffic. It was not
until September that the rains came and
Mardale disappeared once more – perhaps
never to be seen again.

(15) The Measand Falls, Haweswater

On a winter's day ice arrests the Measand Falls
on the western shore of Haweswater. The
flooding of Mardale did not tame this waterfall,
and in times of high rainfall it is spectacular.
Although in full view of the many who use the
road on the other side of the lake, the falls are
rarely visited. They are accessible only by the
footpath which runs the whole length of the
steep western shore of the lake.

(16) Swindale

The wild craggy head of Swindale is one of the
loneliest places in the Lake District. It lies just
to the south of Haweswater, but it is difficult
of access by car and even when Haweswater
was crowded in the drought of 1984, it
remained quiet. The Old Corpse Road which
climbs steeply out of the Haweswater valley
descends almost as steeply into Swindale Head.
As this was only the first section of the long
journey to Shap for burial, such expeditions
must have been daunting.

(17) Waterfall in Swindale

This is one of a long series of falls which brings
the beck down from the Mosedale moorland
into Swindale. These are splendid waterfalls,
but because of their remoteness they are very
little visited.

(18) The Cop Stone

On Moor Divock, the wild upland south east of
Pooley Bridge, there are numerous prehistoric
remains, the most prominent being the Cop
Stone, the one stone still standing of an
ancient stone circle. In the background are the
distant Pennines. The Cop Stone is not far from
the route of the Roman road which, mounting
steadily to the ridge, gave High Street its name.
The whole of Moor Divock has a primeval
atmosphere. Even when the Romans came this
way, the Cop Stone must have been an ancient
relic.

(19) Winter in the Lake District

The scene looking up Ullswater is of the Lake
District at its most threatening. A formidable
range of high mountains fills the horizons,
with the Helvellyn ridge in the centre. It is seen
here from the ancient boundary stone on
Heughscar Hill, a wilderness area to the north
of Ullswater. Few people come this way.

The North

Keswick is the centre for northern Lakeland. Nearby is
Derwent Water, and across the lake are the ridges of Cat
Bells and Maiden Moor. At its head Borrowdale closes in.
To the north is Skiddaw, rising impressively above the
town. The mountains here are of Skiddaw Slate, their
smooth profiles quite different from those of the craggy
central mountains of the Borrowdale volcanics. In the
sixteenth and seventeenth centuries Keswick was an
important mining town, important enough to justify
bringing in miners from Germany who, perhaps for their
own safety, lived on an island in the lake. Now Keswick's
principal industry is tourism. Hugh Walpole made his
contribution to this when, in a house overlooking
Derwent Water, he wrote his Rogue Herries novels, and
turned the tiny hamlet of Watendlath into a place of
pilgrimage. Bassenthwaite Lake, in its wide basin, marks
the northern extremity of the Lake District. Thirlmere, on
the way to central Lakeland, lies deep in its trough below
Helvellyn.

(20) Blencathra

Blencathra – for obvious reasons known also
as Saddleback – rises like a banner proclaiming
the entrance to the northern Lake District. Its
majestic symmetry is typical of the Skiddaw
Slate mountains which form the ridges of this
part of the Lake District. It is seen here across
the 'tundra' above Matterdale, where the road
runs north from Ullswater.

(21) Castlerigg Stone Circle

Did prehistoric man have an eye for scenery?
For Castlerigg Stone Circle is not just an
impressive monument, its setting is superb. It
is seen here against Blencathra. From its other
side the Helvellyn range would be the
backdrop. The Circle consists of forty-eight
megalithic stones in the shape of an oval about
100 feet by 109 feet. Archaeologists are of the
opinion that these were so aligned to act as a
stone calendar.

(22) Brandlehow, Derwent Water

It is spring in the Lake District and a track wanders through the bluebells in the oak woods of Brandlehow on the shores of Derwent Water. This was the first National Trust property in the Lake District, and one of the first National Trust properties in England. The Brandlehow track is part of a footpath network which encircles most of Derwent Water.

(23) Derwent Water

The view across the lake is towards the
Newlands Valley. On the left is the ridge of
Maiden Moor and Cat Bells, the latter being a
favourite climb for young and old. To the right
rises Causey Pike with its distinctive dimple.

(24) Skiddaw

Skiddaw seen from the eastern shore of
Derwent Water in autumn, with cloud just
touching its summit. Skiddaw is the perfect
endpiece for the lake. Indeed the Skiddaw ridge
is the northern endpiece of the Lake District
itself, and beyond stretches the Solway plain.
The dark knoll of The Dodd, planted by the
Forestry Commission, is in the centre. Ullock
Pike rises behind it.

(25) Autumn beside Derwent Water

Even when Keswick is crowded, peace can be found on the shores of Derwent Water. As a speed limit of ten miles an hour operates, the lake itself is quiet. Launches call at jetties on both sides of the lake and there are rowing boats and modest motor boats for hire. Derwent Water remains an unsophisticated lake, and all the better for it.

(26) Derwent Water: looking north

From the eastern shore, looking down the
lake, Rampsholme Island is in the centre, and
away in the distance there is a glimpse of
Bassenthwaite Lake. There can be no better
way to spend a day than to hire a rowing boat
and explore the lake and its islands. Except for
Derwent Island, where there is a house, there
is access to all the islands. Rampsholme Island
is the perfect place for a picnic lunch.

(27) The bridge at Watendlath

This bridge carries the bridleway which, rising
steadily, goes over to Rosthwaite in
Borrowdale. The tiny village of Watendlath,
lying in a fold of the hills above the eastern
shore of Derwent Water, was made famous by
novelist Hugh Walpole as the home of his
heroine, Judith Paris. Under the bridge the
Watendlath Beck hurries on its way to plunge
spectacularly down the Lodore Falls.

(28) The Jaws of Borrowdale

The River Derwent, rising in the high central
mountains, makes it way through the Jaws of
Borrowdale to the lake. At this point the river
and the road are tightly confined between the
precipitous face of Castle Crag and the steep
sides of Grange Fell.

(29) Tarn at Leaves

This, one of the most unfrequented of tarns, is
high on the Borrowdale fells. There are
fascinating places to explore in this rocky,
little-visited area. The names themselves are
intriguing – Bessyboot, Hanging Haystacks,
Cop Knott and Great Hollow.

(30) Derwent Water

Through the reedbeds at the foot of the lake,
the River Derwent goes on to flow into
Bassenthwaite Lake. Rising serenely above is
the Skiddaw ridge – Skiddaw summit in the
centre, with Little Man to the right.

(31) Bassenthwaite Lake

From its eastern shore, the mountains at the
head of the lake are already remote.
Bassenthwaite Lake is the northern outpost of
the Lake District. It is the only 'lake' in the
Lake District, all the others being either 'meres'
or 'waters'. Although the busy A66 runs near
its western shore, this eastern shore and the
lake itself are wide and tranquil. There is a
yachting club at its outflow, and rowing boats
and canoes can be hired.

(32) Summer on Bassenthwaite Lake shore

Beyond the lake rises the Skiddaw massif –
Skiddaw summit on the left, the rocky ridge of
Ullock Pike is in the centre, and The Dodd to
its right. Ullock Pike is the most interesting
way to climb Skiddaw, and the least used.

(33) Castle Rock

Castle Rock stands sentinel at the junction of
St John's Vale with the main road running
south from Keswick to the central Lake
District. It is a popular climbing crag and from
its summit, which can be easily reached by a
footpath, there is a splendid view down the
length of St John's Vale to Blencathra.

(34) St John's Beck, Thirlmere

Near Bridge End Farm, stepping stones cross the St John's Beck. This is the beck which flows out of Thirlmere and then north down St John's Vale. In the centre against a cloudless sky is Great Dodd. The Sticks Pass mounts the steep shoulder on its right to go on to Ullswater.

(35) Helvellyn across Thirlmere

Seen from the Armboth footpath on the quiet western side of Thirlmere, Helvellyn rises impressively above the narrow waters. Thirlmere has been a reservoir for nearly a hundred years and in times of low rainfall its arid rim can give it an air of desolation. In addition, the conifer plantations with their straight boundaries are uncharacteristic of the region. Nevertheless, Helvellyn is probably the most popular mountain in the Lake District.

(36) Birks Stone, Thirlmere

Birks Stone is prominent in the landscape from the minor road which skirts the western shore of Thirlmere. From this huge glaciated outcrop the view is across the head of the Thirlmere valley to Dollywaggon Pike, the southern end of the Helvellyn range. From here the conifer plantations give the area an almost Norwegian atmosphere which is not unpleasing. In recent years there has been some planting of broad-leaved woodland by the Water Authority. In addition, a new footpath has been made along the western shore where once access was strictly forbidden.

The Centre

South of Dunmail Raise the Lake District opens out.
Below is the Vale of Grasmere, ahead lies Windermere,
to the west the Langdale Pikes. This is the most popular
part of the Lake District. In summer Grasmere, a pleasant
village in a lovely setting, has more visitors than is good
for it. Perhaps Wordsworth is responsible for this.
Windermere caters for the tourist. There are sailing clubs
and motor boat clubs beside the lake, sailors and water-
skiers on it. Speedboats roar down it, launches chug
around it, and in the season steamers laden with visitors
sail its whole length. Windermere is an elegant lake,
eleven miles long, but slim. At its narrowest point a ferry
crosses. On its shores stand houses built by the rich in
Victorian times. When new they were ostentatious on
the open lakeside, now they are screened by mature
trees. Save for the Round House on Belle Island, most of
these houses now have other uses: hotels, out-of-door
pursuit centres, visitor centres, and headquarters for
bodies concerned with the countryside. Bowness Bay is
the busiest place on Windermere, but the views from it,
down the lake to its wooded shores, up to its mountain-
ringed head, are unchanged. The Langdale Pikes beckon:
theirs is the best-known mountain profile in England.
And those looking for peace and quiet can find it at
Kentmere, the dale a few miles east of Windermere.

(37) Dunmail Raise: loooking northwards

Dunmail Raise marks the boundary between north and south Lakeland. The summit of the Pass is the 'great divide'. It is said, with some justification, that the weather differs on either side. It is even suggested by some locals that the people on either side differ, too. The large number of drumlins, here catching the autumn sunshine, are evidence of the glacier that ground its way through this centre of the Lake District in the Ice Age.

(38) Helm Crag

Helm Crag, popularly known as The Lion and
the Lamb because of the distinctive form of its
summit crags, rises on the right from the
Greenburn valley. Greenburn, although in the
centre of the Lake District, is a remarkably
secluded and little-frequented dale. It offers a
much quieter and more interesting route up
Helm Crag than the over-used path from the
other, the Easedale, side. From the foot of
Greenburn, the Vale of Grasmere opens out to
the right.

(39) Grasmere: the lake

The view across Grasmere from Loughrigg
Terrace is one of the most popular in the Lake
District. In this unspoilt pastoral scene it is
easy to forget that the village of Grasmere,
invisible in the trees, is busily dealing with its
tourist trade. In the centre is Helm Crag, its
rocky summit just protruding against the
profile of Steel Fell. To its right is the wide
scoop of Dunmail Raise, with the shoulder of
Seat Sandal sweeping up from it.

(40) Bluebells on Grasmere's island

Wordsworth and his family often visited this, Grasmere's only island. It can still be visited and remains a quiet and private place. The island and the whole of the lake shore can be explored by hiring a rowing boat from the little boating station at the head of the lake. Grasmere is a shallow lake, there are reedbeds where wildfowl nest, there are waterlilies, and at its outfall, under Loughrigg, there are lovely shingly beaches.

(41) Grasmere village from Grey Crag

Grasmere village, set in its wide green valley,
is backed by shapely mountains and on the far
horizon, left of centre, are the Langdale Pikes.
St Oswald's Church in the centre of Grasmere
is solid and austere; probably little different
from when Wordsworth used it. The poet's
grave, fittingly modest, is in the churchyard.
Although the names of Grasmere and
Wordsworth are inseparable, Grasmere has
another claim to fame – the Grasmere Sports.
In August each year many thousands
congregate to watch the traditional Lake
District games of fell-running and Cumberland
and Westmorland wrestling. The Sports are
held in the field at the bottom left of the
picture.

(42) Alcock Tarn

Alcock Tarn lies in its rocky cradle high above
the Vale of Grasmere. A footpath from Town
End winds up to this typical Lake District scene
of crag and water. Beyond the Tarn the fells
run up to Heron Pike and on to the Fairfield
Horseshoe.

(43) Dora's Field, Rydal

Behind St Mary's Church at Rydal is Dora's
Field, so called because Wordsworth planted
daffodils here for his favourite daughter, Dora.
Glimpsed through the trees, Rydal Water lies
quiet in its sheltered bowl. Though Dove
Cottage is most closely associated with
Wordsworth, it was in a house near here, at
Rydal Mount, that the poet spent the last
thirty-seven years of his life.

(44) The Langdale Pikes

The Langdale Pikes provide what is certainly
the best-known mountain profile in England.
It is visible from afar. On the much-used
approach from the south the Pikes come into
sight well before Windermere is reached. They
are seen here from the footpath on the south
side of the Great Langdale Beck. The Langdale
Pikes are perhaps too popular. Erosion
problems in Stickle Ghyll necessitated the re-
routeing of the footpath. Now even the new
footpath is becoming eroded.

(45) Pike of Stickle

Pike of Stickle rears steeply out of Mickleden, the final stretch of the Great Langdale valley. The long gully to the right of the Pike is the site of the Axe Factory, where Neolithic man found an extremely hard rock which, after being polished and shaped, made an effective axe. The word 'factory' is appropriate. The axes were widely exported and have been found in many distant places. The 'rejects' can occasionally be found in the long scree that falls at a daunting angle into the valley.

(46) Little Langdale

Little Langdale is south of Great Langdale and parallel to it. With its secluded tarn, Little Langdale is sheltered and quiet, but at its head there is a formidable mountain barrier. Through it, by way of the high Wrynose Pass, a road makes its way westwards to the Duddon valley. This was the route the Romans used when building the road between their Ambleside and Hardknott forts. In places this road can still be traced. In the centre, snow-streaked, is Blake Rigg.

(47) Orrest Head, Windermere

Orrest Head, a rocky knoll high above
Windermere, is a short, steep walk from
Windermere railway station. From it there is
an impressive panorama over the northern
reach of Windermere into the central
mountains. The Langdale Pikes are to the left,
with the snowy slopes of High Raise and Steel
Fell to their right.

(48) Early morning from Ferry Nab, Windermere

This view south from Ferry Nab is of a peaceful lake, but in summer Windermere is often busy with craft of many kinds. From here to Ferry House on the opposite shore is the narrowest part of the lake, and a ferry service operates throughout the year. In summer lake steamers make their way from Waterhead to Lakeside at the far foot of the lake, but even in high season this part of Windermere can be quiet.

(49) The Round House, Belle Island

This is a unique house in a unique setting.
Built in the late eighteenth century on
Windermere's largest island, then without
trees, the house was initially much criticized
for its prominence in the scene. Two hundred
years later it stands among delightful woods.
Belle Island was named after Belle Curwen.
The Curwen family have owned the Round
House almost since it was built, and still live
there. It is not now open to the public.

(50) Western shore of
Windermere

On this the western shore of Windermere are
long secluded footpaths. Some thread their
way along the water's edge, others climb up
steep wooded slopes from which there are
extensive views. All are quiet and
unfrequented. It is difficult, in such places, to
reconcile this aspect of Windermere with the
busy scene at Bowness Bay on the other side
of the lake.

(51) Windermere in winter

The stormy waters of the lake are deserted,
and in the distance the snow-crested Fairfield
Horseshoe rises above Waterhead.
Windermere is more than 200 feet deep in
many places, and its shores shelve steeply into
the water. In winter Windermere has its own
private visitors. The Golden Eye duck flies here
from Scandinavia, and Whooper swans,
uttering their distinctive call, drop in on their
way back to Iceland.

(52) Windermere from
Gummers How

Gummers How is a rocky knoll rising above
the southern reach of Windermere. On this
day of high summer the lake is dotted with
yachts and other craft. Beyond the wooded
western shore of the lake the long backcloth of
mountains includes the Coniston range, the
Langdale Pikes, High Raise and Steel Fell.
The gap to the right is that of Dunmail Raise.

(53) Stott Park bobbin mill

This bobbin mill is on the western side of
Windermere just north of Newby Bridge. Built
in 1836, it has recently been restored to its
original condition and is now open to the
public. In the nineteenth century there were
many bobbin mills in the Lake District, all
powered by the swiftly descending becks and
rivers. To ensure an adequate supply of power
many dams were built in the higher reaches,
and thus new tarns were created. Stott Park
bobbin mill built its dam, appropriately named
High Dam, on the rocky shelf to its west. It is
now an elevated tarn, and a pleasant place to
visit.

(54) High Dam

High Dam, on Finsthwaite Heights, was
constructed to provide water for Stott Park
bobbin mill; now it is a quiet secluded tarn for
the discerning visitor. In 1973 it was acquired
by the National Park Authority, thus ensuring
that there was public access to it, and a
footpath encircles its wooded shores.

(55) Town Head, Troutbeck

North of Windermere, in the Troutbeck valley,
is the little hamlet of Town Head. Behind it
rises the imposing ridge leading on to High
Street. In the centre are the shapely peaks of
Froswick and Ill Bell.

(56) Kentmere

Kentmere in its imposing cirque of mountains
is the first view of the Lake District when
approaching from the south. The valley is a
cul-de-sac, the road finishing at the church.
Beyond this is only the medieval bridleway
which, mounting to the Nan Bield Pass at the
valley head, then descends into the
Haweswater valley. On the skyline is Ill Bell
with Froswick to its right. This is the western
section of the Kentmere Horseshoe, a high
route which, taking in High Street and Harter
Fell, encircles the head of Kentmere.

(57) Pack Horse bridge, Kentmere

This ancient packhorse bridge spans the infant River Kent. Rising from the steep crags below High Street, the swift River Kent in earlier times powered a great number of mills – bobbin mills, paper mills, woollen mills, snuff mills, gunpowder mills – on its way to Morecambe Bay. The River Kent gave Kendal its name, and its industry. The mountains on the skyline, Ill Bell and Froswick, now look down on a quiet and often unfrequented dale.

The South West

Tarn Hows on the road to Coniston is the Lake District in miniature – a small lake encircled with a footpath that old and young can walk, a wooded shore, a shingly beach, and all surrounded by miniature crags. But the views from these crags are wide and splendid. Nothing miniature about them. To the south the Coniston range is against the sky and Coniston Water placid below. Ruskin liked the look of the Coniston mountains and built his house on the eastern shore of the lake to enjoy them. It is open to the public now. Arthur Ransome used Coniston as the background for his children's book, *Swallows and Amazons*. But Coniston's past was different. The district was pitted with copper mines and scarred with quarries, and Coniston Water, now a peaceful lake graced with the steam yacht *The Gondola*, was an industrial highway in those days. Even today there is, on the face of Coniston Old Man, the Bursting Stones Quarry. Far to the south of the lake is Furness Abbey. Though not truly Lake District either in its surrounding or its character, the Abbey was, in past centuries, an integral part of it. And south of Furness Abbey are the treacherous sands of Morecambe Bay, an old route to the Lakes.

(58) Tarn Hows

Tarn Hows on a late autumn day – on the left against the sky is Coniston Old Man with its first dusting of snow. Tarn Hows has a unique charm. Its small scale and its attractive setting make it extremely popular, yet it remains unspoilt. The motor car is banished to car-parks strategically sited in the woodland to the south, and the Tarn and its shores are left in peace.

(59) Tarn Hows in winter

Although the narrow road to Tarn Hows is
hazardous in snow, many people make their
way here since it freezes before the lakes and
the lower tarns. In its beautiful setting it
provides the ideal place for ice skaters, both
experts and beginners. Family parties,
complete with sledges, take possession of the
snowy slopes around the tarn, while others
come to enjoy walking on its frozen surface as
a change from round its shores.

(60) Wetherlam

Seen from the Tarn Hows road to Coniston, the
Tilberthwaite valley leads into the mountains.
Wetherlam is against the sky to the left, with
Yew Tree Farm, backed by the steep slopes of
Holme Fell, in the middle of the picture. This
is a fine example of a traditional Lake District
farm and its spinning gallery is still intact.

(61) Peel Island, Coniston Water

Peel Island lies a short distance from the eastern shore of Coniston Water. It featured as Wild Cat Island in Arthur Ransome's children's book, *Swallows and Amazons*. On this side of the lake a narrow road winds is way between woodland and lake shore. There are many shingly beaches on the lakeside and secluded car-parks in the woodland. There is a speed limit of ten miles per hour on the lake and the only powered vessel likely to be seen is *The Gondola*, the stately steam yacht, once derelict, which the National Trust restored some years ago. It sails at regular times round the lake, calling at a pier near Peel Island. The profile of Coniston Old Man is on the left.

(62) Coniston Water

This is the view looking north from high above
the eastern shore of Coniston Water. Perched
above the head of the lake is the craggy face
of Holm Fell, while Wetherlam rises
majestically to the left. The village of Coniston
can be glimpsed just left of centre.

(63) The Coppermines valley, Coniston

The Coniston district bears ample evidence of its former industries and nowhere are these more noticeable than in the Coppermines valley. The remains are everywhere. It is a scarred valley but nevertheless has a certain fascination. The massive shoulder of Coniston Old Man is against the skyline on the left, Swirl How is in the centre. The youth hostel at the head of the dale is one of the few buildings of the Coppermines complex remaining intact.

(64) Levers Water and Swirl How

Levers Water lies high on the Coniston fells
locked in by crags, one of which is named,
appropriately, The Prison. Swirl How, part of
the ridge linking Coniston Old Man and
Wetherlam, is on the skyline. Levers Water is
in fact a reservoir. The modest weir at its
outflow was built in the days when the
Coppermines valley below was a busy
industrial centre.

(65) Coniston Old Man from Torver Common

The abandoned quarry in the foreground is one of a number on Torver High Common. This is now a wilderness area, very little visited, lying south of the Walna Scar track linking Coniston with the Duddon valley. Coniston Old Man is on the skyline. There is still quarrying in this district. Though not visible from here, the Bursting Stones Quarry on the east face of Coniston Old Man can be seen from many miles away.

(66) Kelly Hall Tarn

This pleasant tarn is on the top of Torver Back
Common just above the western shore of
Coniston Water. In the view, just left of centre,
is Dow Crag with the formidable crags which
are a favourite resort for rock climbers.
Coniston Old Man is to the right and in the
deep coomb between them lies the small tarn
of Goats Water. The Walna Scar track goes
straight across the middle distance.

(67) Furness Abbey

The ruins of Furness Abbey, built in red
sandstone and set in a sheltered site on the
Furness peninsula, are well south-west of the
Lake District. The monks of the twelfth century
shunned the tangle of wilderness and water
which was then the Lake District and chose
sites for their abbeys on the fringe of it: Shap
Abbey, Holm Cultram Abbey, Calder Abbey,
and most important of all, Furness Abbey. It
became one of the wealthiest Cistercian
establishments in the country, second only to
Fountains Abbey. Much of this wealth came
from the Lake District, where the Abbey
owned huge tracts of land, thousands of sheep,
and both copper and lead mines.

(68) The Kent Estuary

The River Kent rises in the steep crags at the
head of the Kentmere valley. Its outflow is here
in the flat expanse of the Kent Estuary and
Kents Bank is across the water. To the right
lies the vast expanse of the treacherous, ever-
changing sands of Morecambe Bay. In past
centuries the accepted route to the Furness
peninsula and southern Lake District was
across these sands from Hest Bank near
Morecambe to Kents Bank. Not everybody
reached Kents Bank.

The West

The West is the nether region of the Lake District, and for the more discerning. It lies between the barrier of the central mountains and the Cumbrian coast. The way to it is circuitous but the rewards are ample. The first of these western valleys, Dunnerdale, is narrow, and up it a scenic road, closely following the River Duddon, threads its way to the Wrynose Pass. From Dunnerdale the way to Eskdale is over Birker Moor, and from this high road there are extensive views of the western faces of the Lake District's highest mountains. The Eskdale Valley has Harter Fell above it and at its head the western escarpment of the Bow Fell and Crinkle Crag range. To its north lies Wasdale. Wasdale is the most dramatic valley in the Lake District, some would say in all England, with its crag-ringed head, Great Gable rising imperiously in the centre, and its lake, Wastwater, cold and forbidding. It is, justly, the symbol of the Lake District National Park. Ennerdale is a quiet, almost a private lake, its upper reaches locked in by Pillar Mountain. Crummock Water and Buttermere are jewels among lakes, set off by shapely mountains. And at Buttermere, to look across the head of the lake to the high mountains on the skyline is to look back into the heart of the Lake District.

(69) The Duddon Valley

On a frosty winter morning Seathwaite Bridge,
and indeed the whole of Dunnerdale, is
deserted. The narrow bridge, just north of
Seathwaite village, carries the road up the
valley to mount steadily to the Wrynose Pass.
The Duddon Valley is considered by many to
be the most beautiful in the Lake District and
the road runs parallel to the river for most of
its way, sometimes high above it, sometimes
by its side.

(70) Duddon Iron Furnace

The eighteenth-century Duddon Iron Furnace,
long abandoned, ruinous and engulfed in
vegetation, was recently partly restored by the
National Park Authority and is now open to
the public. In this essentially rural setting it is
difficult to envisage how different the scene
must have been when the Furnace was in use.
Now the woodland which once was coppiced
to fuel it has closed about it.

(71) Hardknott Castle Roman fort

The north-western gate of this Roman fort
looks out across the deep declivity of Eskdale
to the Scafell range. This is certainly the most
dramatically sited Roman fort in England. The
remains, which are extensive, are adjacent to
the Hardknott Pass road that runs up steeply
from Eskdale and for the motorist is the most
daunting road in the Lake District. The
Romans used this route as the only way to link
the fort at Ambleside with that of Ravenglass
on the west coast. In this inhospitable place, at
a height of 800 feet, they built an extensive
fort, not a crude outpost. The ruins cover
about three acres, the site was properly
drained and there was a bath house.

(72) Eskdale

The village of Boot lies in its green pastures in
central Eskdale. Rising above it to the left is
Harter Fell. The road, here threading its way
quietly up the dale, is bound for the steep and
perilous Hardknott Pass. In the centre of the
picture is Hows Wood, a mixture of natural
woodland and conifer plantation. This has
recently been bought from the Forestry
Commission with the intention of removing
the conifers and replanting with broad-leaved
woodland. It will then be open to the public.

(73) Wasdale

The head of Wasdale, with Great Gable to the
left and the Scafells, England's highest
mountains, against the skyline on the right.
Wasdale has a special claim on the affections
of the British people: it was here that
mountaineering and rock climbing were born,
and in the Wastwater Hotel at the head of the
dale, now frequented by the mountaineers of
today, there hang photographs of the men
who pioneered the first routes and of the rock
faces which they scaled.

(74) Wastwater: the Screes

Wastwater is without doubt the most dramatic lake in England. The Screes, seen here dark against the blue waters, have a menacing beauty and a path threads its precarious way across them to the head of the lake. The road running along this western shore has a bend known as Echo Corner, where it was the habit, in earlier times, for the coachman to stop and crack his whip. And after a moment of silence, back across the lake would come the echo. This was used to some effect ten years ago when Wastwater came under threat. British Nuclear Fuels unveiled proposals to extract more water from the lake for its Sellafield works. A party of objectors assembled at Echo Corner and, at a given signal a rhetorical question was asked: 'Should more water be taken from Wastwater?' The orchestrated answer was a resounding 'No'. After a few seconds of complete silence the echo came back perfectly, 'No'. It was as though the lake and the mountains themselves had spoken. Perhaps it was prophetic for when the decision came through after a lengthy public inquiry, it was 'No'.

(75) England's deepest lake

The western shore of Wastwater with
Yewbarrow on the left and Great Gable, cloud-
capped, in the centre. Wastwater is the deepest
lake in England with the Screes plunging
down into 260 feet of water. It is a quiet, some
would say a desolate, lake in a wild setting. No
powerboats are permitted on it, and because of
the frequency of sudden gusts of wind down
the dale there is little sailing.

(76) Great Gable

The noble cone of Great Gable rises above the
May blossom at Wasdale Head. Great Gable is
not the highest mountain in the Lake District,
but it is the most commanding. It attracts both
walkers and climbers. Perhaps it is too
popular. The steep and rocky ascent from Sty
Head to the summit cairn is now badly eroded.
Rock climbers favour the Girdle Traverse to
reach the climbing crags of this its western
face, of which Napes Needle is deservedly the
most famous.

(77) Ennerdale

The prospect up Ennerdale Water towards
Pillar at the head of the valley is one of the
finest lake and mountain views in all England.
No building stands on the shore of the lake and
there is no public road beyond its entrance. It
must be explored on foot. Although the conifer
plantations of the Forestry Commission extend
well up the dale, and the lake has long been
used for water supply, Ennerdale is today a
supremely lovely place.

(78) Gathering the flock in Ennerdale

A pastoral scene near the shores of Ennerdale Water. It is at Bowness Knott, prominent in the scene, that the motor road finishes: a car-park is tucked discreetly into the trees at its foot. On the horizon is Pillar Mountain in the centre, with Pillar Rock, a favourite with rock climbers, against the sky. To its right is the sharp peak of Steeple and the ridge of Scoat Fell.

(79) Fleetwith Pike

Fleetwith Pike rises imperiously from the tree-fringed head of Buttermere. Below its distinctive shoulder the road runs up steeply to the Honister Pass. The top of the Pass is deeply scarred with quarry workings but, at 1190 feet, it is a convenient place from which to explore the higher mountains, among them Haystacks, Green Gable, and, for the strenuous, Great Gable.

(80) Buttermere

Haystacks across the head of Buttermere. This
lake, set like a gem in its cirque of mountains,
is considered by many to be the most idyllic in
England. About a mile long, its waters are
placid and serene, its shores well wooded, and
there are pleasant footpaths all round the lake.
Buttermere is, however, no mere shallow pool,
it is deceptively deep. Its bed is the glaciated
trough that, before silt built a barrier, made
one lake of what are now Buttermere and
Crummock Water.